HOW TO SUPERCHARGE

YOUR CONFIDENCE

CHRISTINA NEAL

circus

HOW TO SUPERCHARGE YOUR CONFIDENCE

An Hachette UK Company
www.hachette.co.uk

Circus Books, an imprint of Summersdale Publishers Ltd
Part of Octopus Publishing Group Limited
Carmelite House
50 Victoria Embankment
LONDON
EC4Y 0DZ
UK

www.summersdale.com

Printed and bound in China

ISBN: 978-1-78783-513-9

Substantial discounts on bulk quantities of Summersdale books are available to corporations, professional associations and other organizations. For details contact general enquiries: telephone: +44 (0) 1243 771107 or email: enquiries@summersdale.com.

10 9 8 7 6 5 4 3 2 1

For Dave C. Every day is an adventure
With thanks to Howard Cooper, Alec Lom and Brad Burton

CONTENTS

INTRODUCTION

A positive mindset can go a long way to making a difference to what you can achieve, and of course, how you feel about yourself. Even sitting down to write this book could be viewed in two different ways. I could see the prospect as a daunting task and delay getting started. Or I could view it as a great opportunity to write about a topic that I feel passionately about – improving your confidence.

Whatever your goals or ambitions, you need to have a reasonable amount of confidence and self-belief. If you don't truly believe in your abilities, you won't have the confidence to pursue your ambitions. Or when setbacks occur, you may tell yourself you're not capable and you'll quit. So, what can you do when you're plagued with self-doubt about completing a task or project? This book will show you how to adopt a more positive mindset, banish doubts, improve your self-belief and build your confidence step by step.

We will also explore the power of the mind and how it can help or hinder. We will explain how to take control of your thoughts and how to adopt a clear mindset to give you the confidence to move forward. Having a positive mindset is key, but many people are battling mental health issues. According to NHS Digital, one sixth of the population in England aged 16 to 64 has a mental health problem at any one time. And mental health issues seem to be a worldwide concern. According to Mental Health America (a community dedicated to helping those with mental health issues), over 44 million adults in the US are reported to have a mental health condition, and the rate of young people experiencing a mental health condition is on the rise. We will also reveal how to identify triggers that can cause anxiety and how to deal with them.

This book will also show you how to adopt a healthy attitude and provides the lowdown on various therapies and treatments that exist to help you lead a more positive, fulfilling life.

FIRST STEPS

CONFIDENCE

IS THE
COMPANION
OF SUCCESS.

GETTING CONFIDENCE-READY

Firstly, take a moment to think about where you are now in life. Are you happy with your lot? Are you in control of your life, your health and your emotional well-being? Here are some quick and easy ways to start building your confidence:

- Write down a list of everything you have achieved – a quick bullet point list is fine.

- Think of exams you've passed, or obstacles you've overcome that you didn't think you'd be able to.

- Think of compliments you've received in the past from friends and colleagues.

- Let go of past mistakes – don't harbor regrets about things you wish you'd done differently or hadn't done. You've learned from them, now move on.

- Focus on what you're good at – and keep doing it.

- Push yourself out of your comfort zone – sign up for a fitness challenge or a course where you can learn a new skill.

- Offer yourself constructive advice – don't let a negative inner voice put you down. Be good to yourself – tell yourself you can do things, rather than telling yourself you can't. Be an ally to yourself.

There is only one corner of the universe you can be certain of improving, and that's your own self.

Aldous Huxley

BREAK DOWN TASKS

If you are struggling with your emotions and feeling
overwhelmed, take some time to think about why this is.
If it's because you feel you have too many things going
on in your life at once, such as having to juggle a busy
job with looking after someone, then look at how you
manage your time. If certain tasks seem overwhelming,
break them down into small chunks. Decide what
comes first then work through them one by one.

Although this book is about improving your confidence and
leading a more fulfilling life, remember you don't have to
make massive changes to your life overnight. You can commit
to one or two small changes or actions each day that will add
up and get results. You might decide to get up half an hour
earlier every day and start work earlier, or you might decide
to go to bed half an hour earlier every night. In a typical
week, that'll mean you'll have an extra 3.5 hours' sleep.
Seemingly small things can add up to make a big difference.

BE AWARE OF YOUR VOCABULARY

Using positive self-talk is the way
to grow your confidence account.
Be positive in the language you use.
Example: "I have a great new job
I'm excited about" rather than "I'm
nervous about starting a new job".

BANISH DOUBT BY TAKING ACTION

What can you do when you're plagued with self-doubt about completing a task or project? Just get started. It sounds so simple and it is. Even if you're not sure if it's the right way forward, you'll work it out as you go along. There's no golden rule to say you can't change direction at a later stage. Don't let fear cripple you.

The most
effective
way
to do it
is to do it.

Amelia Earhart

LISTEN
TO YOUR
THOUGHTS

It's important to understand how your thinking patterns affect your confidence, so that you can manage negative thoughts and not let them hold you back. Take some time to reflect on how you have been speaking to yourself. Has your inner voice been constructive, helpful and supportive, or have you been beating yourself up? Would you speak to a friend in the same way that you have been speaking to yourself? Try to get your inner voice under control. When you hear yourself thinking a negative thought or telling yourself you're not slim/fit/good enough, tell that inner voice to shut up. Or you can simply recognize the fact that your inner voice is there, and that it's being critical, and just accept it as a thought. Thoughts are just thoughts, they aren't necessarily reality.

Trust your instincts and your abilities. You are bound to be capable of far more than you think.

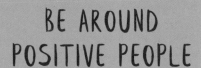

BE AROUND POSITIVE PEOPLE

Surround yourself with people who are upbeat, energized and supportive and their optimism will rub off on you.

OTHER PEOPLE'S OPINIONS

Even those who have a responsibility for our welfare or are closest to us can negatively influence our subconscious. Maybe you've never believed you can cook thanks to particularly quelling criticism from your teacher when you were young. Perhaps your sibling used to make hurtful comments about your appearance. Supercharging your confidence means identifying when your negative self-perception comes from someone else's subjective opinion and is not a true measure of your worth and ability.

Ultimately the greatest help is self-help.

BREAK AWAY FROM BAD SOCIAL MEDIA HABITS

Social media can have a negative impact on our confidence levels. Many people only share flattering (and edited) photos on social media. People tend to share their achievements rather than daily struggles. We're encouraged to be fit, young and successful. No wonder we feel like we've underperformed when life throws up challenges. Motivational coach Brad Burton orchestrated a social media experiment – he once posted a photo of himself on Facebook collecting a new BMW worth $130,000 to give the impression that he was rich. He then revealed that appearances can be deceiving and explained that he had actually rented it just to create the post. Brad wanted to break the illusion that coaches and leaders have perfect lives and deep pockets.

A journey of a thousand miles begins with a single step.

Lao Tzu

EMBRACE
THE UNKNOWN

Stepping out of your comfort zone
from time to time and trying new
things will boost your self-belief.

BE YOURSELF.

Everybody else is already taken.

Oscar Wilde

THE
POWER
OF YOUR
MIND

BELIEVE IN YOURSELF

You may have heard the famous quote from Henry Ford, "Whether you think you can, or you think you can't, you're probably right." Believe in yourself and you can achieve great things.

HAVING FAITH
IN YOURSELF,
EVEN WHEN IT
SEEMS NO ONE
ELSE DOES,
IS THE KEY TO
BUILDING
CONFIDENCE.

BE POSITIVE
AND CONSISTENT

A positive mindset and consistent action will usually
get you where you want to be, but if you don't truly
believe in your own abilities then you'll lack motivation
to commit 100 per cent to your ambitions. The first sign
of any setback and you'll be tempted to quit. You must
believe in yourself even if others don't. Remember
their motivations may not be genuine if they are
critical. They may not want you to succeed because
they are envious or scared of losing you.
Don't get bogged down by negativity.

TRY MEDITATION

Meditation is a great way to calm the mind when you start overthinking or worrying about things. Find a quiet place and focus on your breathing: concentrating on this one thing will push other, disruptive thoughts out of your head. Deep breathing also allows more oxygen to enter your lungs, which is good for our immune systems as a good oxygen supply protects the body's cells.

BELIEVE IN YOURSELF AND NOTHING WILL STAND IN YOUR WAY.

LEARN TO RECEIVE COMPLIMENTS

When someone pays you a compliment, look them in the eye. Don't look surprised or dismiss their praise. Thank them.

CHOOSE YOUR
COMPANY CAREFULLY

The people around you should encourage and support you. If you tell someone you are going to change career or take up a new hobby, they should be supportive and offer their encouragement and not scoff at your ambitions. You should feel energized in their company. Make the right choices with the company you keep and you'll be around people who inspire and motivate you.

USE OTHERS' ACHIEVEMENTS FOR INSPIRATION

People who have achieved incredible things against the odds can inspire you to believe in yourself. If they can do it, so can you. It's never too early or too late in life to achieve goals that matter to you. Here are some great examples:

- At just 17, football star Pelé was shocked when he was called to play for Brazil during the World Cup in 1958. In a recent interview, the star said he thought it was a mistake when he was told he was selected for the team. He went on to score twice for Brazil during the team's 5–2 win over Sweden, becoming the youngest player ever to appear in the World Cup final.

- At the age of 32, author J. K. Rowling secured her first book deal. She started writing at the age of 25 so she had pursued her idea for seven years. At the time of securing her first book deal, she was a penniless, recently divorced single mom. Her first book was rejected by 12 publishers before Bloomsbury agreed to publish it.

- KFC founder Colonel Harland Sanders was 65 years old when he started the fast-food chain. He felt sure that people would love his fried chicken recipe even though he had received over 1,000 rejections before the first KFC franchise was opened in Salt Lake City in 1952.

- Fauja Singh started running at the age of 81 after losing his wife and has completed multiple marathons. In 2003, at the age of 92, he completed the Toronto Waterfront Marathon in 5 hours 40 minutes.

TRACK YOUR PROGRESS

If you are trying to complete a certain task or goal such as losing weight, make a note of what you did well and how you are progressing. It will keep you motivated. Writing down what you did will help you to understand what is working and what isn't, so that you can make changes or adjustments as you go along. It will also keep you motivated, as seeing your tasks written down will make you realize just how much you've accomplished and how far you've come.

Believe in yourself
and everything
else will follow.

PRACTICE BEING CONFIDENT

When you meet someone new, shake
their hand firmly and make eye
contact. First impressions count.

BEING SMART WITH YOUR TIME AND TAKING ACTION

YOUR BIGGEST ENEMY IS YOURSELF

- SO BE YOUR BEST FRIEND.

BUILD CONFIDENCE GRADUALLY

If you don't feel particularly confident right now, then know that confidence and self-esteem can be developed. Taking action will help your confidence grow. Setting goals and sticking to them will help you feel like you're taking control.

FIND A MENTOR

If you have a goal in mind, find
someone you can bounce ideas off
who can guide you. Learn as much
as you can from their experiences.

Never underestimate the power of Passion.

Eve Sawyer

TAKE
CONSISTENT ACTION

This may sound simple, but you can build your confidence simply by taking action and getting things done. The more tasks you accomplish, the more confident you will feel. It's like putting money into a savings account. Work on your "confidence account" by banking (accomplishing) tasks. Confidence comes from taking action. Don't put things off. Every time you say you're going to do something, and you put it off, your confidence can be negatively affected.

SET MINI-GOALS

This is a great way to build
confidence gradually. Start
with small, achievable goals
and as you achieve them,
your confidence will grow.

CRAFT A
MORNING ROUTINE

A morning routine will give you structure and purpose. It will also give you a sense of "owning the day", rather than the day owning you. It's all too easy to wake up and find yourself at the mercy of emails or internet distractions, losing productive hours in the process. You can develop a morning routine that will help you get more things done by picking four things you think will help you focus. Many high achievers swear by exercising first thing – it boosts blood and oxygen flow to the brain, which will help with concentration, and it will help you start the day on a positive mental note too. Get up and drink a glass of water, then start the day with a 10- to 20-minute burst of exercise – a brisk walk or jog – write a quick to-do list of essential tasks, and get stuck into your list, crossing items off as you do them.

LISTEN TO OTHERS CAREFULLY

We often make mistakes and misunderstand others because we are so busy thinking of what we're going to say next instead of listening. Be an active listener. Don't just hear what people are saying, absorb the information, as well as the person's tone of voice. If you can listen well, you will understand others clearly and communication will be improved. Listening carefully when learning a new skill will also make you better at that skill, which, in turn, will give you more confidence.

Great things are done by a series of small things brought together.

Vincent van Gogh

BE MORE METHODICAL

Make a to-do list, then prioritize and work through each task in order of priority. It may sound so simple, but the very act of writing things down will give you focus and purpose. And the satisfaction you'll get from being able to tick things off as you go through them will help build your confidence account. The more you feel in control of your life and schedule, the more your confidence will grow.

GET BETTER AT
KEY TASKS

The more competent you are at certain tasks, the more confident you will be. Improve your skills and become more proficient at a given task or role. This will boost your confidence. Make time to perfect your skills or practice a new skill. For instance, maybe you feel your computer skills could be improved. There's a wealth of free online tutorials on every aspect of using a computer. Set aside 15 minutes every day to learn how to get better at using a computer or certain software that would make your life easier by allowing you to accomplish more or work more efficiently.

GOALS

WRITE DOWN GOALS

The act of putting pen to paper, or finger to keyboard, will help to reaffirm your goals. Write your goals down and keep them where you can easily see them, such as on your phone, on the fridge, in a diary or notebook you refer to regularly. This creates a strong form of motivation as it will be a constant reminder of your goals. It's also important to make sure your goals are ones that genuinely motivate you – they should be your goals and no one else's. Your goals should be about doing things you want to do because they mean something to you on a personal level. In other words, you're not doing things to gain approval or external validation or reward from others.

SPEAK SLOWLY AND CLEARLY

Don't mumble quietly or let your words
tumble out. Speak clearly and concisely
and people will be more inclined to listen.
You're more likely to be interrupted if you
speak quietly or people can't hear you
clearly. Being interrupted is not good for
self-esteem – there's nothing worse than
feeling that you're not being heard.

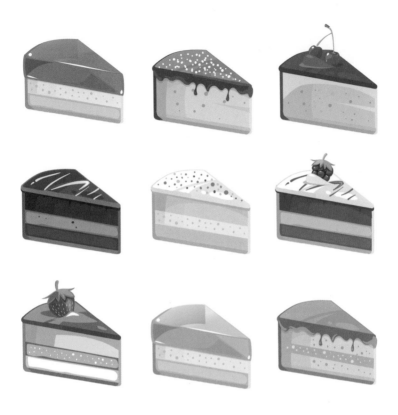

TAKE RESPONSIBILITY

Don't blame others for things you did or didn't do. If you
meant to go for a run but you didn't because your friend
invited you to go shopping, it was your choice. No one has
the ability to force you to do something. People may try to
cajole you to eat the cake or "have one more drink" but if you
don't want to do it then don't let them change your mind. If
they truly respect you, they will respect your wishes. And if
they don't, they may be trying to sabotage your efforts. Do
you really want to give them control over your actions?

LEARN HOW TO SAY NO

Many of us find it so much easier and less stressful to say yes to something we don't want to do rather than stand our ground. But agreeing to something we don't want to do can make us resentful and self-critical. It can also affect your confidence, as deep down you will feel like you're not assertive enough to speak your mind. You may have a clear reason in mind for turning down an invite, but you don't have to give an excuse or over-explain. If you do give a reason for saying no, keep it short and concise.

YOU ARE ENTIRELY UP TO YOU.

DON'T BE TOO HARD ON YOURSELF

You don't have to be perfect. Just do your best and give yourself credit for the things you do well and the things you're working at.

DRAW ON
YOUR STRENGTHS

You may be confident at certain tasks and lack confidence in other situations. Accept that this is OK and draw strength from things you are accomplished at doing.

Focus on being productive instead of busy.

Tim Ferriss

DON'T LET OTHER PEOPLE DISTRACT YOU FROM GETTING THINGS DONE

If you're a sympathetic person and a good listener, people may lay all their problems on you, even if you're too busy to listen or you have a lot on your own plate. You start the day with the intention of accomplishing key tasks but find yourself sidetracked by a friend who wants to share their problems. Don't get into long-winded personal conversations if you're busy. Tell the person you want to be there for them, but you have to get a certain task done and it would be best if you could speak later.

DON'T GET DEMORALIZED

Remember that anything worth doing will be difficult at some point. Obstacles may arise, but this means your achievement will feel all the more amazing when you accomplish your goal.

LIFE HAS NO REMOTE.

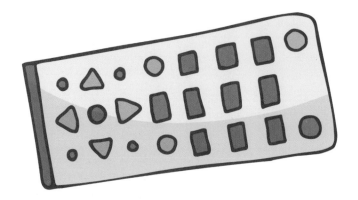

GET UP AND CHANGE IT YOURSELF.

Mark A. Cooper

DON'T COMPETE
WITH OTHERS

As the saying goes, "Look in the mirror – that is your only competition." We all have different skills and talents – someone you perceive to be better than you at a certain task may have been doing it longer or have had training you haven't had, so don't try to compete. The only person you have to compete with is you. Aim to continually better yourself – be more productive or informed than you were last week and the week before that. As you learn and develop your skills, your confidence will grow.

SURPRISE YOURSELF AND SAY YES!

When it comes to taking action, it's easy to do things we feel comfortable with but every now and then, push yourself out of your comfort zone. Say yes to something you wouldn't normally agree to do. It could be running a 10K, taking up a new sport or hobby or anything that pushes you to extend your boundaries. You'll develop your confidence by trying out new tasks and realizing that you have the ability and skill to learn new things.

OVERCOMING ANXIETY

AS SOON AS YOU TRUST YOURSELF, YOU WILL KNOW HOW TO LIVE.

Johann Wolfgang von Goethe

WHAT IS ANXIETY?

Anxiety may be holding you back. Anxiety is a term for when a person feels fear, stress, apprehension, nerves and worry. It can also involve worrying about a situation disproportionately. While fear of what lies ahead, or the unknown, can be perfectly natural (such as apprehension about starting a new job, for example), constant and extreme feelings of fear and worry can mean you have an anxiety disorder. Speak to your doctor or health professional and seek help if these feelings persist.

I can't change the direction of the wind, but I can adjust my sails to always reach my destination.

Jimmy Dean

STEER AWAY FROM NEGATIVE NEWS

Watching negative stories on the news can cause stress and anxiety. If watching or listening to current affairs is causing you stress, take a break from listening to or watching anything reporting bad or distressing news.

TALK TO SOMEONE

Talk things through with a friend or close colleague. Speak to someone who has had a similar experience to you who you know will understand. Sharing your problems and how you feel you are coping with a trusted friend or family member is a relief and will give you a chance to work through any issues you are experiencing.

TAKE DEEP BREATHS

This may sound like simple advice but can be very effective at reducing anxiety. Breathe in for 4 seconds, hold for 2 seconds, then out for 6 seconds. This helps you slow down your breathing rate and relax.

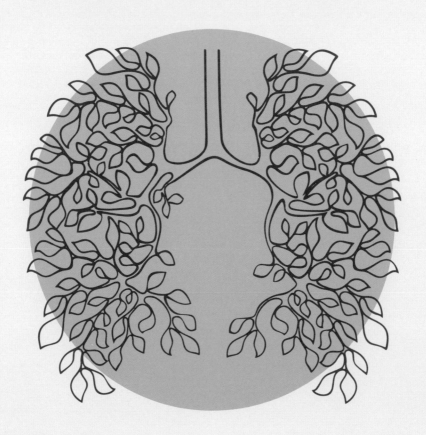

One important
key to success is
self-confidence.
An important key
to self-confidence
is preparation.

Arthur Ashe

DELEGATE AND SAY NO

Taking on too much work or responsibility and worrying too much about others can cause anxiety. If you feel you are doing this then sit down and work out what you can delegate at home and at work and learn to say no to others' requests. Be strong. If you haven't got time to do something or help someone out, have the courage to say so rather than putting yourself in a situation where your stress levels could increase.

CHALLENGE
NEGATIVE THOUGHTS

Next time a negative thought creeps into your head, question it. You
may think you're not good enough at your job or as a partner. Ask
yourself to find specific reasons why you think that's the case, and
see if you can come up with one. If you think you're not good enough
for your partner for instance, question it. Rather than focusing on
a belief that you're "not good enough" for someone else, think of
all the good things you've done for them and how you've supported
them. Write down three good things you've done for that person.
If that fails, there is an expression: "Don't believe everything you
think." Remember not to give too much power to negative thoughts.

MAKE EYE CONTACT

When talking to others, look them in the eye. Direct eye contact suggests confidence and also demonstrates that you are showing genuine interest in others. In many countries, like the US, eye contact is seen as a mark of respect. It is also taken as a sign of sincerity and can help you appear more confident. A study from the Idiap Research Institute in Switzerland showed that people in senior positions at work look longer at their colleagues. The study also revealed that eye contact shows a person's dominance in a conversation.

SHOW YOURSELF SOME RESPECT

The way you talk to yourself can have a significant effect on your confidence. You wouldn't let anyone else be rude to you, so why do it to yourself? It's easy to fall into the trap of telling yourself "I'm too fat", "I'm not clever" or "I'm not attractive". You wouldn't tell a friend they were fat or not smart so why say these things to yourself? Show yourself respect and consideration. Be a friend to yourself. When you need to make a decision, think about what advice you would give a friend if they were in the same situation.

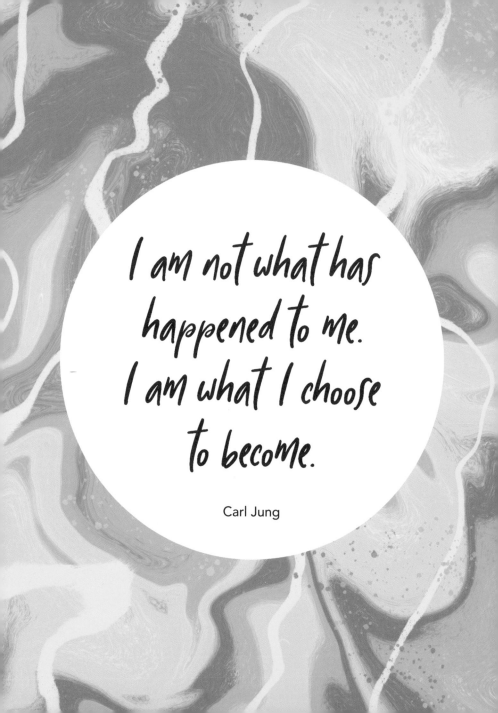

I am not what has happened to me. I am what I choose to become.

Carl Jung

USE POSITIVE MANTRAS

Saying, thinking or writing down positive mantras (phrases) is a great way to increase your confidence, although it's important to say them regularly in order for the mind to make a powerful connection to them. Examples include: "I am strong and grounded", "I love and honor myself" or "I can do anything I put my mind to achieving".

KEEP A DIARY

If you suffer from anxiety, the mental health charity Mind recommends keeping a diary and making a note of what happens when you feel anxious or think you may be having a panic attack. This may help you spot a pattern in what triggers these experiences, so that you can notice early on when they are starting to happen.

USE PRACTICAL OPTIMISM

Try to be optimistic, even when things are tough. Optimism will propel you forward and help you develop your self-belief. Being optimistic will help you to take action rather than dwelling on things going wrong.

WHATEVER YOU CAN DREAM, YOU CAN DO.

DON'T LET FEAR
HOLD YOU BACK

Fast forward to an elderly version of you. Imagine how you would feel if you hadn't tried to achieve your goals. If you are nervous about trying something new, like quitting your job and setting up your own business, or embarking on a new adventure, write down a list of key things you have achieved. This will help give you confidence to pursue your goals and dreams.

DON'T
OVERTHINK
THINGS

Sometimes you can drive yourself mad
with worry and anxiety wondering about
what will happen if something goes wrong.
Don't overthink things. If you are worried
about something, acknowledge that it's
normal to have fears and doubts but don't
let them hold you back – accept they are
there and get on with what you want to
do. In short, make a plan and stick to it.

USE A STRONG
TONE OF VOICE

When you talk to and interact with others, say things like you
mean them – have a firm and definite tone of voice, even if you
don't always feel particularly confident about what you're saying.
If you speak in a nervous, high-pitched broken tone or too quietly,
the person you are speaking to may not take you seriously. When
giving a presentation at work or speaking in public, speak in
a controlled and firm manner and you will project confidence
and authority, even if that's not what you're feeling inside.

USE YOUR IMAGINATION

The mind is an incredibly powerful tool and many coaching experts believe that your unconscious mind can't tell the difference between something you are imagining vividly and reality. So if you imagine yourself succeeding at a task or achieving a goal, your brain will then create neural pathways to program you for success. Create a short mental movie of you completing a task or achieving a goal and picture what the surroundings are like. Imagine how things around you look, feel, sound and smell and feel your confidence and excitement growing in anticipation.

BE SOCIABLE

Talk to a wide variety of people
when you're in social situations.
If you feel shy, ask people
questions about themselves.
This usually breaks the ice.

KNOW YOU'RE NOT ALONE

Even people who are seemingly confident have moments of self-doubt. Many even think they're not good enough and are expecting to be "found out" for not being as talented or gifted as people think. "Imposter Syndrome" is a term for when a person doubts their accomplishments and is scared of being exposed as a "fraud". Despite their success, they think they have just been fortunate. Award-winning actress Meryl Streep once reportedly said: "You think: 'Why would anyone want to see me again in a movie? And I don't know how to act anyway so why am I doing this?'" Acknowledging that people who appear confident but underneath have the same doubts as everyone else can help you with your own confidence issues. Remember, we're all human and we all find ourselves in situations where we may lack confidence from time to time.

FIND A POSITIVE
IN ALL SITUATIONS

When you are dealing with a stressful
situation, look for a positive side.
Maybe it's having the support of
a friend or you realizing you're
more resilient than you thought.

SELF-CONFIDENCE IS THE FIRST REQUISITE TO GREAT UNDERTAKINGS.

Samuel Johnson

FINDING POSITIVE ROLE MODELS

EMULATE A ROLE MODEL'S BEHAVIOR

If you want to achieve something or boost your confidence, follow the habits and behaviors of a positive role model. Role models can provide us with a blueprint for living and, by doing so, help us get to the point we want to be at in our lives. Seeing someone else achieve what you'd like to achieve one day shows you that it can be done and gives you something to aspire to. Find out what your role model did to get where they wanted to be and emulate it.

Big ambitions require hard work.

READ ABOUT
HIGH ACHIEVERS

Social media can be a great way to find inspirational quotes and blog posts from business coaches and highly successful people, but it's OK to draw inspiration from successful celebrities too. Madonna's work ethic is indisputable and her ability to keep going when things get tough is well documented. Lady Gaga is reportedly one of the hardest working people in the music business. Reading biographies of famous people you admire and how they achieved their goals will inspire you to keep going when things get tough and remind you that it's possible to get where you want to be even when there are obstacles in your way.

CHOOSE A ROLE MODEL YOU KNOW

It's natural to admire the achievements of celebrities and there's nothing wrong with that, but if you can, also find a role model that is a person you know so that you can look to them personally for guidance and support.

EXCELLENCE IS NOT A DESTINATION BUT A JOURNEY.

HEALTHY BODY, HEALTHY MIND

MAXIMIZE YOUR ENERGY

We talked earlier about taking action and building your confidence account by getting things done. You need energy to accomplish goals. Energy is one of your biggest assets. Exercise will give you energy (so long as you don't overdo it!). The World Health Organization lists the benefits of regular cardiovascular exercise as reducing the risk of heart disease by 40 per cent, reducing stroke risk by 20–40 per cent and reducing the risk of Type 2 diabetes by 30 per cent. Being physically fit will make you look and feel better and give you a sense of self-control. Regular activity can lead to improved concentration, sharper memory, faster learning and prolonged mental stamina.

A healthy outside starts from the inside.

Robert Urich

STAY IN SHAPE

Being overweight can increase your risk of Type 2 diabetes, high blood pressure, heart disease, stroke and liver and kidney problems. It can also affect your confidence and self-esteem and increase anxiety, according to the American website mentalhelp.net. Finally, carrying around extra weight will also reduce your energy levels, so make sure you keep active and eat healthily.

Your confidence is a precious thing. Keep it safe.

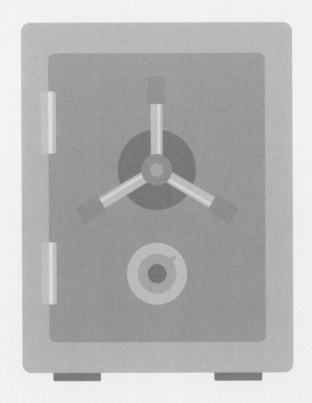

HAVE A HEALTHY DIET

A good diet is not just important for physical
health but also for your mental well-being too,
according to the Mental Health Foundation.
It suggests that diet can play a role in the
management and prevention of various
conditions including depression and ADHD.

DRINK WATER REGULARLY

The human brain consists of around 85 per cent water, so if you aren't properly hydrated it will affect your concentration and increase your risk of headaches. A study conducted by the University of East London and the University of Westminster showed that reaction times were 14 per cent faster in study subjects who were well hydrated compared to those who weren't.

LOOK AFTER YOURSELF

If your health is good, so are your energy
levels, which will give you the drive and
gumption to get things done. You'll be
less likely to start a project or task only
to have to stop due to poor health.
Take care of yourself and your
health and the results will come.

HOW TO EXERCISE

Try to exercise three to five times per week for a minimum of 30 minutes. It's OK to break it down into small chunks – three lots of 10 minutes is just as effective as one 30-minute chunk. Here are some useful tips:

- If you haven't exercised for some time, start gradually and don't expect to be super fit when you first begin. Anything new will take your body time to adapt to. Stick at it, and within four to six weeks you'll start feeling fitter.

- Find a form of exercise you enjoy. Willpower alone is not enough – it's got to be something you can envisage having the motivation to do at least three times a week.

- Work out with a friend. It's a great way to make it more sociable and you'll be less likely to skip a workout, as you won't want to let the other person down.

- Mix it up – variety is key. If you're constantly doing the same thing each time, you're likely to get bored. Try a new exercise class or hire a personal trainer at the gym to devise you a new workout.

- Set yourself a target – decide you're going to walk 10,000 steps each day, get fit for a 5K run or run 2 miles in under 20 minutes. This will bring out your competitive streak and give you something specific to work toward.

Health is
the greatest
gift.
Contentment is
the greatest
wealth.

Buddha

SPEND TIME WITH
GOOD PEOPLE

Spend time with people who are good
for your mental health – people who
are upbeat, supportive and positive.
Their positivity will rub off on you.

CREATE MORE
STRUCTURE IN YOUR LIFE

Have a routine – if you think you'll
be tempted to skip a workout, have
a set time in your diary for doing
it. Choose the time of day that
works best for you and stick to it.

PUT HEALTH BEFORE WEALTH

Working yourself so hard that you feel permanently stressed and exhausted will make you ill in the long term and make it very hard for you to feel positive and confident about life. Put your health before work and remember that it will be hard to accomplish anything if you are ill through overdoing it.

LOOK AFTER YOUR MENTAL HEALTH

If you are an overthinker who tends to look ahead and worry too much about the long term, try to take the focus away from what may or may not happen a year from now and focus on the present. Try to keep things simple by doing one thing you didn't do yesterday or doing something better than you did yesterday. This will stop your mind from getting too busy and being overwhelmed. Your mental health is as important as your physical well-being.

A HEALTHY BODY STARTS WITH A HEALTHY MINDSET.

GET ENOUGH SLEEP

Sleep is incredibly important for emotional well-being as well as physical health. Some of us swear by 8 hours, while other people manage well on 6 hours of good-quality shut-eye. Find out how much sleep you typically need to function at your best and aim to get that amount of sleep each night. If you find you go to bed and lie awake at night with a busy mind, there are some things you can do that may help calm your thoughts, such as meditation or making sure your bedroom has a clear space by removing clutter. There are also various apps you can try to help you sleep, including Relax Melodies, Relax & Sleep and Nature Sounds Relax and Sleep.

TURN OFF TECHNOLOGY

If you are still struggling to sleep, turn off anything electronic so that there are no harsh lights in the room. Make sure your room is caveman dark. The absence of light sends out a signal that it's time to rest.

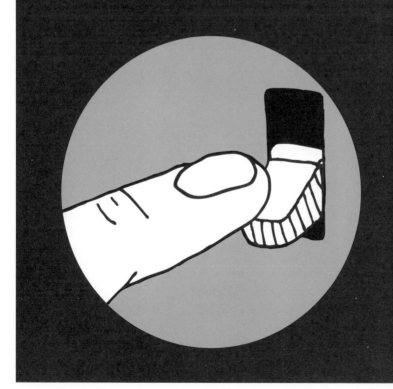

EXERCISE CAN
HELP YOU SLEEP

According to the National Sleep Foundation, just one gentle
exercise session daily (like walking) can reduce the time it
takes to fall asleep, so this is another good reason why it's
worth being active. That said, plan the timing of your exercise
sessions carefully. Exercise can help you sleep but if you exercise
too close to bedtime then it may have the opposite effect.

CUT BACK ON SUGAR

We all know that too much sugar presents health risks. High-sugar diets are linked to heart disease – one recent study of over 30,000 people found that those who consumed 17–21 per cent of their calories from added sugar had a 38 per cent greater risk of dying from heart disease. It can also increase inflammation in the body and cause insulin resistance, both of which increase cancer risk. But did you know there may also be a link between high sugar consumption and low mood? A 2015 study of nearly 70,000 women, published on the *American Journal of Clinical Nutrition*'s website, found greater risks of depression in those with a high sugar intake.

WHAT IF YOU CAN'T SLEEP?

Eat bananas. They contain magnesium and potassium, both natural muscle relaxants, which will help you stay calm. A medium banana contains 8 per cent of your RDA of magnesium and 12 per cent of your RDA of potassium. Magnesium activates the parasympathetic nervous system, which is the system in your body responsible for helping you to relax. Bananas also contain minerals and amino acids that can help aid sleep.

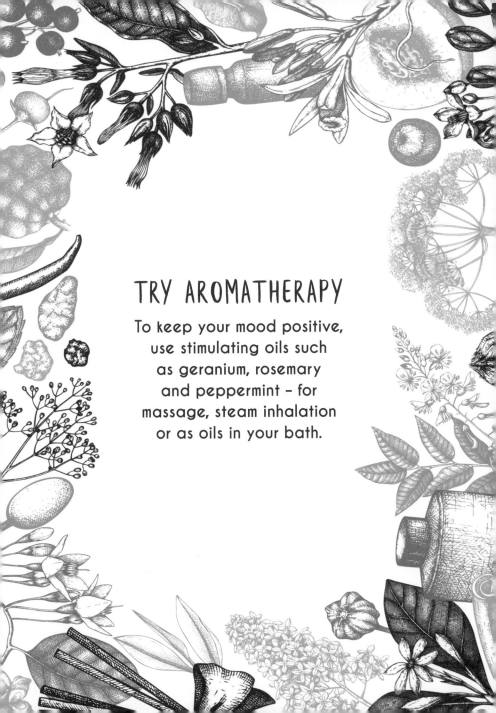

TRY AROMATHERAPY

To keep your mood positive,
use stimulating oils such
as geranium, rosemary
and peppermint – for
massage, steam inhalation
or as oils in your bath.

TAKE CHARGE OF TECHNOLOGY

Technology can easily rob you of a good night's sleep. It's tempting to take your tablet, phone or laptop to bed and end up watching endless videos, trawling through social media or, even worse, answering emails and finishing off work when you're meant be winding down. That last social media update or email with bad news that could have waited until the morning can keep you awake and get your mind buzzing. Create some boundaries around screen time – stop reading messages at least an hour before bedtime to give you time to wind down mentally and switch off.

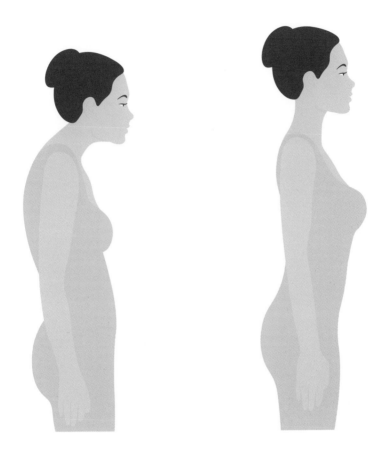

TRY THE ALEXANDER TECHNIQUE

Are your muscles feeling tight? This technique consists of exercises to help improve your posture and get you to stand up straight and tall. Visit www.alexandertechnique.com.

YOUR NET WORTH WILL GROW

WITH YOUR SELF-WORTH.

KEEP YOUR
ENVIRONMENT CALM

Make sure your bedroom is tidy and dark enough to sleep in.
Get rid of clutter like discarded clothing, exercise equipment
and technology such as cables, chargers and wires. According
to the Sleep Council, your bedroom should be a sanctuary – a
calm and relaxed space that is free from gadgets that may
buzz and keep us awake, as well as bright lights, which can
interfere with the body's circadian rhythm (the body's internal
clock that regulates our cycle of biological processes).

HAVE A GOOD LAUGH

When you laugh, endorphins are released,
giving you feelings of happiness. Laughter is
also a good way to keep your blood pressure
healthy. If you feel down, watch a comedy
film or get together with uplifting friends
or family members who make you laugh.

CLOSE OFF THE DAY

If you're worrying about something, make a note of what's
on your mind and write down what you'll do the next day to
resolve it. Or schedule a time to tackle it. Do this early on so you
can spend the latter part of the evening doing things that will
help you relax. Have a set waking time and bedtime, as your
body will thrive on routine and your sleep should improve.

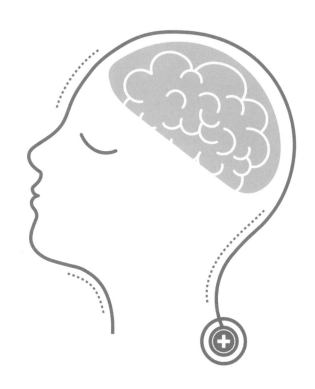

USEFUL THERAPIES AND TREATMENTS

TREAT YOURSELF WITH THE SAME CONSIDERATION

AS YOU WOULD SOMEONE YOU LOVE.

LET'S TALK

CBT or cognitive behavioral therapy is a talking therapy that focuses on behavior, cognition and problem solving. It focuses on the idea that emotions and behaviors are not caused by events but an interpretation of events. CBT is not about focusing on the root of your problems – instead, it's about putting problems or issues into context and making sense of them. It identifies the vicious cycles that are keeping you trapped and finds the best ways to break the cycle. If you are feeling down or have a busy mind, talk to someone about how you are feeling. According to the Mental Health Foundation, talking therapies like CBT will help you learn how to manage negative thoughts and make positive changes.

TRY MINDFULNESS

Medically recognized for improving mood and mental well-being, mindfulness is about living in the moment and being aware of our thoughts and feelings as they occur. Professor Mark Williams, former director of the Oxford Mindfulness Centre, says that seeing the present moment clearly can allow us to positively change the way we see ourselves and our lives.

Don't strive to
be average

"   "

– stand out!

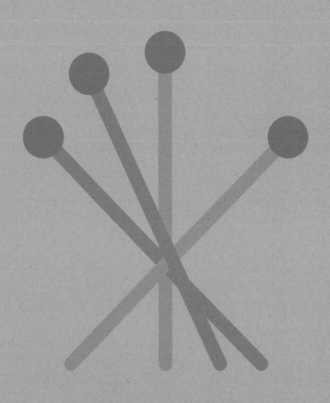

TRY ACUPUNCTURE

If your body feels stiff or sore and you are carrying
a lot of tension, acupuncture could be worth a
try as it can relieve pain. Acupuncture involves
inserting fine needles just under the skin, or
slightly deeper to reach muscle tissue, at certain
sites in the body to improve blood flow to promote
healing. It can treat, among other things, low
back pain, knee pain, neck pain and migraines.

USE VISUALIZATION TECHNIQUES

It sounds simple but visualizing a confident version of you achieving a goal will help you feel more positive. Firstly, write your visualization down, then put yourself in a relaxed environment. Pay attention to your breathing: breathe slowly and deeply, then let go of any tension. Create pictures in your mind that are bright and vivid. Imagine your surroundings – where you are, who is with you and what you are doing. Picture the weather. The more specific you can be, the more effective your visualization will be.

TRY YOGA FOR MIND AND BODY

Yoga is not just about giving your body a good stretch but also balancing body and mind. You can do it at home or in a class and take your time to work out what your body is capable of doing. You don't have to compete with anyone else. Not only will it make your body stronger and more flexible, it will also calm the mind. A 2013 study by Massachusetts General Hospital found that the physiological state of rest induced by yoga postures and breathing techniques helped to generate positive changes in immune function.

TRY BELLY
BREATHING

Deep-breathing techniques can help to restore calmness
to mind and body. (When we're stressed, we tend to
take shallow breaths, which can disrupt the balance
of gases in the body.) Sit down comfortably, place one
hand on your stomach just below your ribcage, then
place your other hand in the middle of your chest.
Breathe in deeply through your nostrils and allow your
first hand to be pushed out by your stomach. Breathe
out through your lips. Repeat up to ten times.

GIVE EFT A GO

EFT (Emotional Freedom Techniques) uses tapping to release blocked energy, improving health and general well-being. Techniques are based on energy moving through the body; blockages can cause illness and emotional issues. EFT involves holding onto a negative emotion or thought that is blocking you while tapping on a body part, then repeating but using a positive statement to replace the negative one. There are plenty of online tutorials that will guide you through the process.

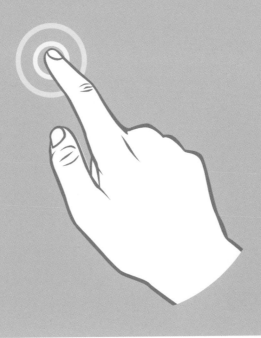

Respect yourself and others will respect you.

TRY REFLEXOLOGY
TO RESTORE CALM

Reflexology uses stimulation of certain points on the feet,
lower legs, hands or face to help the flow of energy in the
body. It works on the theory that these different points
correspond with different areas of the body. It involves
a practitioner stimulating pressure points – usually
in the feet – with their thumb or forefinger to release
energy blockages and allow energy to flow more freely.

INVEST IN
YOUR HEALTH

Taking good care of your
health is the biggest investment
you will ever make.

Self-trust is the first secret of success.

Ralph Waldo Emerson

HAVE A MASSAGE

A regular massage will help relieve stress, improve mood and boost immunity. A 2005 study published on the PubMed.gov website found that women with breast cancer who had a massage three times a week were less depressed and angry. A 2010 study published in the *Journal of Alternative and Complementary Medicine* found that massage helped to increase the number of circulating lymphocytes (white blood cells in the vertebrae's immune system), which can boost immunity.

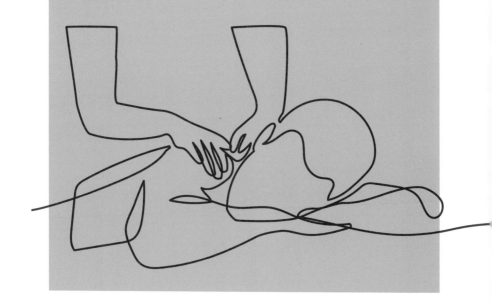

Have faith in yourself

- you know more than you think.

BE MINDFUL

Becoming more aware of your feelings or what's happening in the present moment can help you understand yourself better. You can do this by trying to notice things around you – such as noises and smells – and be more aware of your thoughts. See thoughts as mental events rather than reality.

TRY MINDFULNESS MEDITATION

This means sitting quietly in a peaceful environment, ideally for up to 20 minutes, while paying attention to sounds around you or your breathing and trying to keep your mind focused on the present moment. Take some deep breaths. Each time your mind drifts or wanders onto something else, bring it back to the present moment. If you have a negative thought, or a thought enters your head while you are trying to clear your mind, acknowledge it, then let it go. Your ability to focus on the moment will improve in time.

BE RESPONSIBLE

Remind yourself that you are in
control of your life. Try not to blame
anyone else for things that aren't
right in your life at the moment. Hold
yourself accountable for where you
are today and regain control over
your life. Tell yourself each day:
"I am responsible for my own life."
This enables you to take control
over the life you choose to lead.

LEARN HOW TO SLOW DOWN INTERNAL DIALOGUE

If you suffer with anxiety, you may have lots of different thoughts in your head at once. Often, it's not what you are saying to yourself that's perpetuating the anxiety, it's how you are saying it. Chances are that anxious dialogue is being spoken internally in a very fast and panicked tone. So, if you are feeling anxious, notice your internal dialogue and then consciously slow it right down. Halt 3–5 seconds between each word and notice how this calms your mind.

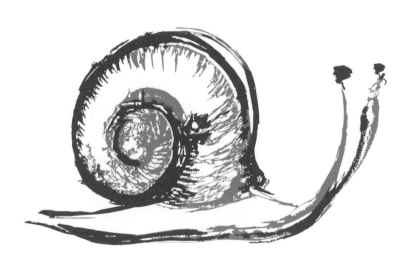

You don't need to compete because nobody can be you.

LIFE ISN'T A COMPETITION

Don't try to compete with anyone else
– the only person you want to improve
is you. And don't try to impress other
people. Just be yourself. Trying to be
someone you're not is tiring, because
you're working to keep up a certain
appearance. It's much less stressful
and more relaxing to be yourself.

FOLLOW YOUR PASSION

It's hugely important to follow your passion because if you pursue something you don't enjoy, you'll probably suck at it! If your heart isn't in something, you'll find it a chore, your motivation will be lacking, and you'll struggle to get it done, whereas we always go the extra mile when we're doing something we love. Follow your heart and do what you want to do in life, not what you feel you should be doing or what your parents or peers think you should be doing.

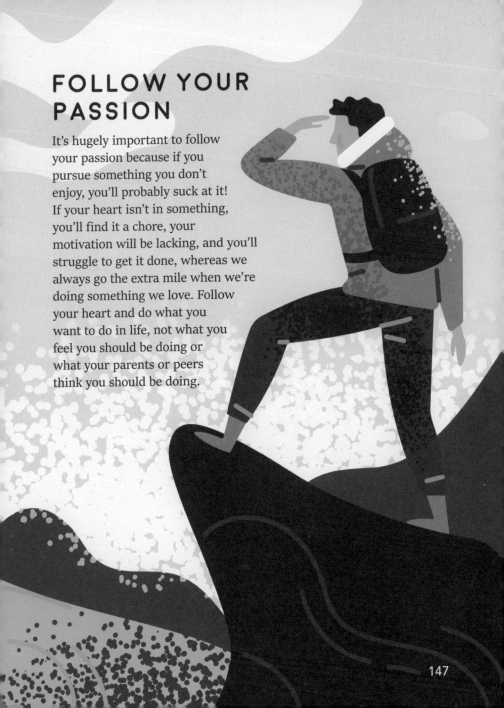

KNOW THAT THINGS HAPPEN FOR A REASON

If something didn't go your way, it might have been for your benefit, even if it doesn't feel like that at the time. As upsetting as it is to lose your job or break up with a partner, you may have been meant for bigger and better things. It's sad when a relationship ends, but then you might find someone else who is a more suitable partner; or maybe you're meant to be alone for a while, which may encourage you to try different pursuits and become more independent.

BE GRATEFUL

Each day take a few minutes to appreciate the good things in your life – even when times are tough. Your health, your partner, your job – anything you value.

Self-worth is determined by you. You don't have to depend on someone telling you who you are.

Beyoncé

RECOGNIZE YOUR STRENGTHS

Know what you're good at. We all have talents and abilities – recognize what yours are and take some time to appreciate having these skills. For instance, you may be a talented artist, good at writing or adept with computers and anything tech. Acknowledging your strengths is good for your confidence.

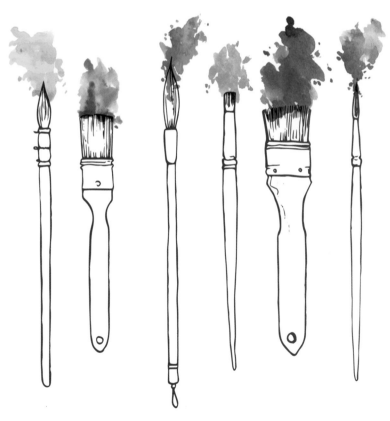

PUT YOURSELF FIRST

If you are a caring person, it's easy to be tempted
to do what others want you to do in order to please
them, but make yourself a priority. Be honest with
yourself about whether or not you'd like to take up
an invite or help someone out. If you don't fancy
it and haven't got time, then say so. Remember:
be yourself – that means doing the things you
want to do and living the life you want to live.

CARVE OUT SOME "ME TIME" EACH DAY

Make sure you have some time in your day to do something you enjoy doing, which makes you feel empowered, relaxed or brings joy into your life. It could be exercise, reading or watching a TV show that you particularly enjoy. Make it your own personal "switch-off time".

ACCEPT LIFE'S CHALLENGES

Life can feel challenging sometimes and it certainly throws curve balls at us but remember that everyone else is probably feeling the same. None of us have all the answers – we're all trying to discover what works and figuring it out as we go along.

BE CURIOUS

Be curious about things in life;
this is a great way to learn.
Don't just accept an answer
or a theory. Question it and
broaden your knowledge.

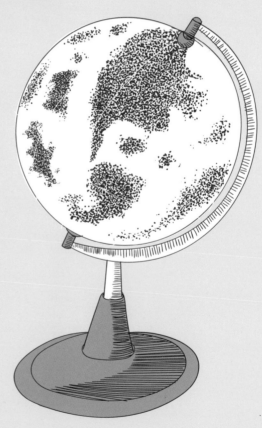

YOU HAVE A CHOICE OVER YOUR EMOTIONS

You may wake up one day and feel tired, then think, "this is going to be a tough day as I'm already worn out." Or you may choose to view things differently and say to yourself: "I'll do my best today and not be too hard on myself as I'm tired, and I'll take the opportunity to have an early night tonight so that I feel good tomorrow." The choice is yours – but adopting a more positive view will help you go about your day more productively. You can't always control what happens to you, but you can control your reaction to situations and events.

FINAL THOUGHTS

Be thankful for what you've got.

Try to see the positive in each situation.

View mistakes as learning experiences.

Don't beat yourself up when
things don't go to plan.

Never give up – start afresh
with a new approach.

Life is a gift – you're here,
so make the most of it!

ABOUT THE AUTHOR

Christina Neal is an experienced writer, editor and published author of several books, notably *Run Yourself Fit*, *Dementia Care: A Guide* and *The World Marathon Book*. She is also the former editor of *Women's Fitness* and *Women's Running* magazines and current editor of *Slim, Fit & Healthy* magazine as well as the founder of Dementia Help, a free online resource for family carers (dementiahelpuk.com).

Christina thrives on achievement and personal development and is also an accredited life coach, a qualified personal trainer and a regular runner who has completed two marathons. She lives and works in Essex, UK, with her partner Dave and her cat Binky. You can follow Christina on Twitter @chrisfitneal or get in touch with her by email at c.neal@mac.com.

IMAGE CREDITS

Have you enjoyed this book?
If so, why not write a review on your favorite website?

If you're interested in finding out more about our books,
find us on Facebook at **Summersdale Publishers**
and follow us on Twitter at **@Summersdale**.

Thanks very much for buying this Summersdale book.

www.summersdale.com